So You Want To Work In

Healthcare?

Margaret McAlpine

Editor: Kay Barnham
Inside design: Peta Morey
Cover design: Elaine Wilkinson

Published in Great Britain in 2004 by Hodder Wayland,
an imprint of Hodder Children's Books.

This paperback edition published in 2008 by Wayland

British Library Cataloguing Publication Data
McAlpine, Margaret
So you want to work in healthcare?
1.Public health – Vocational guidance – Juvenile literature
I.Title
362.1'023

ISBN 9780750254878

Picture Acknowledgements. The publishers would like to thank the following for allowing their pictures to be reproduced in this publication:
Tom Stewart / Corbis 4, 7, 29, 37, 39, 56; Norbert Schaefer / Corbis 5, 28; Ralph A. Clevenger / Corbis 6; James A. Sugar / Corbis 8; Ed Bock / Corbis 9, 43 (bottom); David Woods / Corbis 12, 26; Jose Luis Pelaez Inc / Corbis 13, 16, 17, 21, 33, 36, 41, 53, 55, 57, 59; Strauss / Curtis / Corbis 14; Corbis 15; Stephen Welstead / Corbis 19 (left); Bernardo Bucci / Corbis 19 (right); Gary D. Landsman / Corbis 20; Michael Heron / Corbis 22, 23, 30; Jon Feingersh / Corbis 24, 35 (top), 48; Ed Wheeler / Corbis 25; Steve Prezant / Corbis 27; Lester Lefkowitz / Corbis 31, 54; Helen King / Corbis 32; Warren Morgan / Corbis 35 (bottom); Tom & Dee Ann McCarthy/ Corbis 38, 40, 58; R.W. Jones / Corbis 43 (top); Bill Miles / Corbis 44; John-Marshell Morgan / Corbis 45; John Henley / Corbis 46; Michael Keller / Corbis 47, 51 (top); Randy Faris / Corbis 49; Chris Gupton / Corbis 51 (bottom); Roy Morsch / Corbis 52; Peter Beck / Corbis 11.

Printed in China

Wayland
338 Euston Road
London NW1 3BH

Wayland is an imprint of Hachette Children's Books, an Hachette Livre UK Company.

Note: Photographs illustrating the 'day in the life of' pages are posed by models.

Contents

Words in **bold** can be found in the glossary.

Dentist

What is a dentist?

Dentists treat diseases and conditions of the teeth, gums and mouth. They also teach their patients how to look after their teeth. People who always clean and floss their teeth are less likely to develop serious problems.

Dentists also deal with dental injuries, such as chipped or broken teeth. Some illnesses can affect the condition of a person's teeth. Regular check-ups mean that dentists can keep things under control.

Specialist dentists called orthodontists correct the position of teeth.

Dentists work in hospitals, clinics and in private **practices**. Many are self-employed. Usually, dentists work as part of a team that includes dental nurses and dental hygienists.

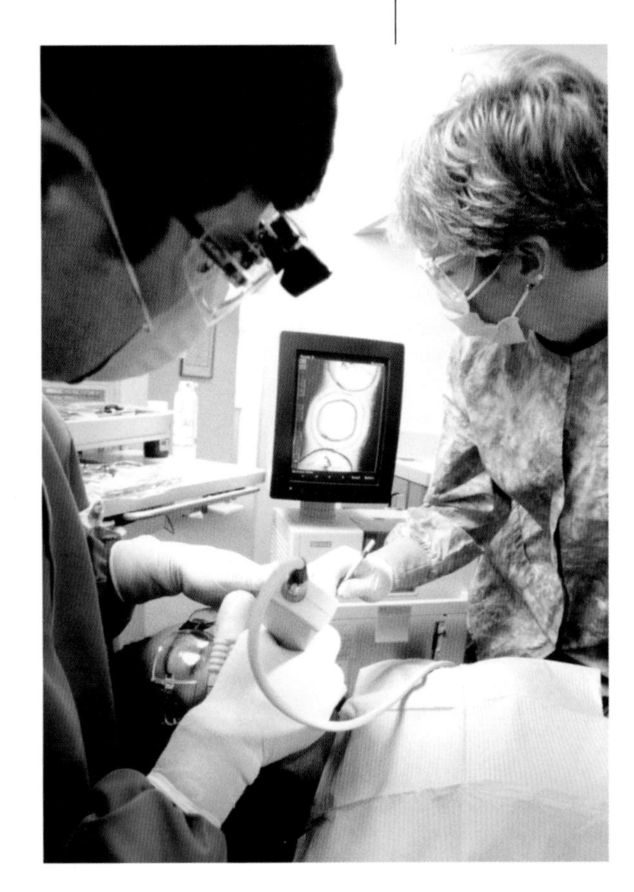

Dentists work as part of a team.

Ancient teeth

Human beings have always suffered from painful teeth. The remains of Ancient Egyptians have been found with holes drilled in their teeth. This treatment was probably carried out to relieve the pain of abscesses – cavities filled with pus.

Eating less sweet, sugary food helps keep teeth healthy.

The dental nurse is there to help the dentist. Her job includes:

- Writing down any comments the dentist makes while checking each patient's mouth and teeth.
- Setting out the equipment needed to treat a patient.
- **Sterilizing** instruments.
- Preparing the material for fillings.

The dental hygienist's job includes:

- Cleaning a patient's teeth by **scaling** them to remove tartar, plaque and stains.
- Polishing teeth to make sure they are as white and sparkling as possible.
- Giving advice to patients about caring for teeth and keeping them in good condition.

Main tasks of a dentist

A dentist's main task is to look after their patients' teeth, inspecting them regularly for signs of decay or disease.

If teeth are to stay healthy, they need to be cleaned thoroughly. Some dentists scale and polish teeth themselves, while others hand the work over to a dental hygienist.

However, even teeth that are well looked after can become decayed. When this happens, dentists remove the bad part of the tooth and put a **filling** into the cavity, or hole. If the root of a tooth becomes infected, dentists can remove it using special instruments.

Dentists can repair teeth that are damaged or broken. Each tooth is filed down and a new piece – called a **crown** or a **cap** – is fitted over the top.

A few months or years spent wearing braces can result in a lifetime of straight teeth.

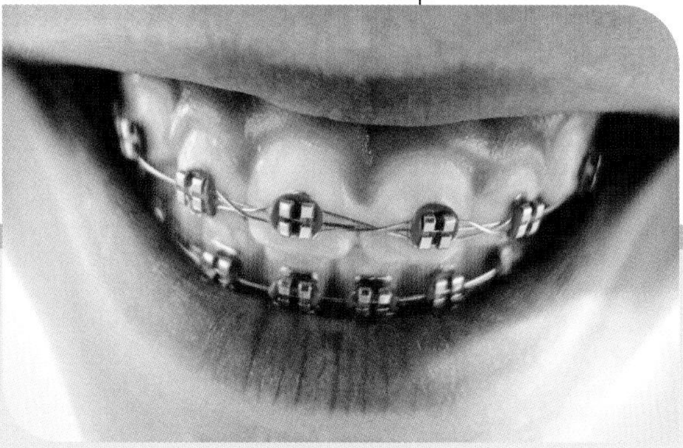

Good points and bad points

'I try to make my surgery a pleasant place and do my best to help my patients relax.'

'It's very satisfying seeing a patient leave with a dental problem solved. However, my job can be difficult when a patient is really frightened of receiving treatment.'

When teeth are too badly damaged to repair, dentists pull them out and then take measurements so that replacements can be made. **Dentures** are false teeth attached to a plate that fits inside the mouth. If fewer teeth are missing, false teeth are fastened between healthy teeth – this is known as a bridge. A dental laboratory makes the dentures or bridges. Then the dentist makes sure that the new teeth fit.

Dentists take **X-rays** of their patients' mouths so that they can see exactly what is going on beneath the surface of the teeth and gums. They give patients local **anaesthetics** to make sure that they feel no pain during treatment.

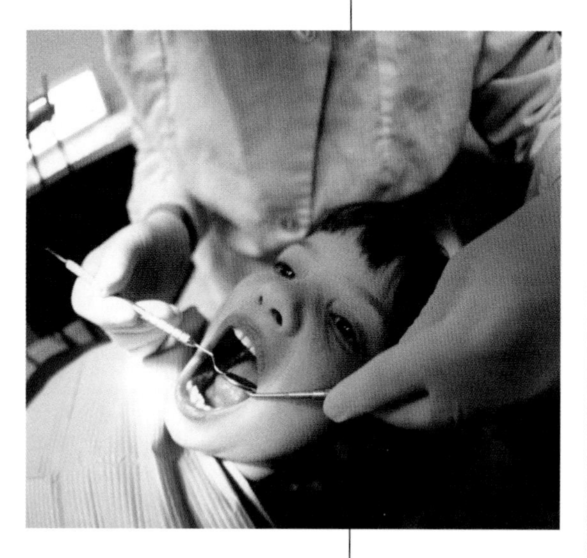

A dental check-up starts with an examination of the patient's mouth and teeth.

Orthodontists specialize in straightening uneven or crooked teeth. They use braces – wire devices that are fitted round the teeth. Over time, braces are slowly adjusted, pulling the teeth into shape.

Some dentists work in hospitals. They perform surgery such as:

- correcting a patient's cleft palate (a hole in the roof of the mouth);
- rebuilding a patient's mouth after damage caused by an injury, an operation or illness.

Other dentists carry out research into dental problems, such as tooth **decay**.

Skills needed to be a dentist

Scientific knowledge
Dentists need to have a high standard of scientific-knowledge about how the body works and how to treat teeth.

A steady hand
Dentists work with sharp instruments, so their hand movements need to be very accurate. A wrong move could cause both pain and damage to their patients.

A strong stomach
Dentists cannot afford to be squeamish. They have to cope with a certain amount of mess, including blood and saliva.

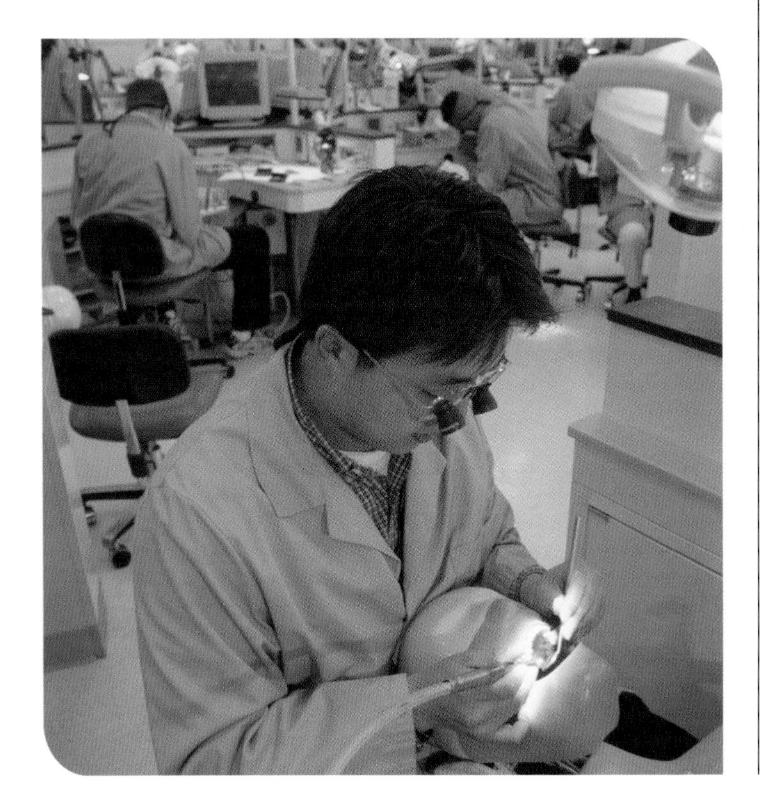

There is a great deal to learn before a student qualifies as a dentist.

Children are encouraged to look after their teeth.

fact file

It takes a long time to become a dentist – at least five years. First, students need three 'A' Levels (in chemistry, physics and biology) or five H grades if they are studying in Scotland. Then they learn all about the human body and how it works. They also develop and practise dentistry skills, such as filling and pulling out teeth.

Patience

It can take a long time to make a nervous patient feel relaxed. Dentists have to be prepared to move slowly, explaining exactly what will happen during the treatment and answering any questions. Trying to hurry things along can result in a patient becoming frightened, upset and difficult to treat.

Friendliness

Dentists need to be warm and sympathetic to put patients at their ease.

Business skills

Dentists are often self-employed. To run their own business, they need to be organized and keep clear records and accounts.

A day in the life of a dentist

Andrew Brown

Andrew qualified as a dentist six years ago. He and three other dentists work together in a dental partnership. They share receptionists, dental nurses and hygienists.

9.30 am A family comes in for a check-up. The two children have had regular check-ups since they were tiny and their teeth are well looked after. They are keen to chat. I examine everybody's teeth and then the mother has a scale and polish.

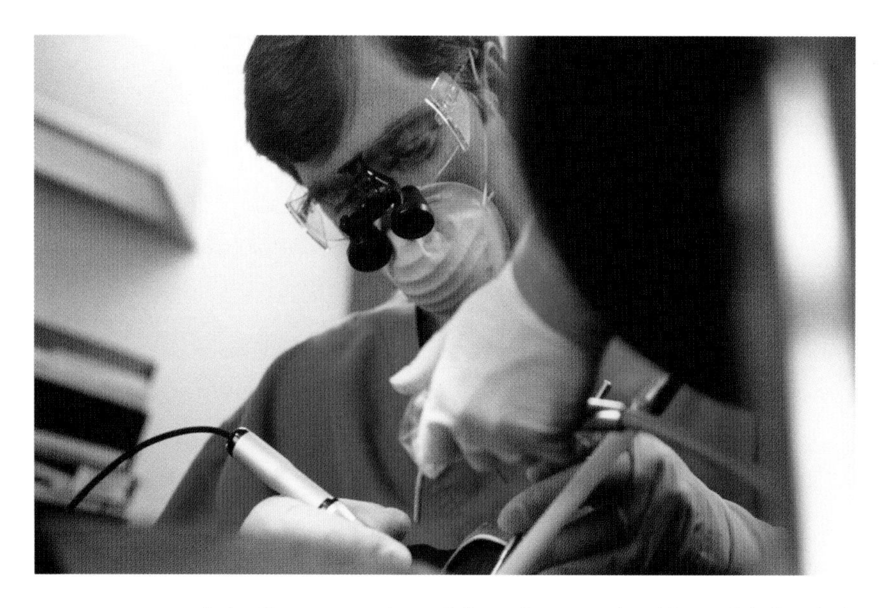

A dentist must work carefully and accurately with special electrical equipment.

10.15 am My second patient is not so easy. He stopped visiting the dentist when he left college and – after a gap of five or six years – there's quite a lot of work to be done. I'm seeing him every two or three weeks to carry out repair work.

11.15 am Time for a cup of coffee.

11.45 am I look at some X-rays before my next patient arrives. She is twelve years old and is having trouble with her teeth. When the patient arrives, we look at the X-rays together. I explain that I would like her to see an orthodontist who specializes in straightening teeth.

12.30 pm I update patient records on my computer.

1.30 pm Lunch – and a chance to read a dental journal to keep up with new developments.

2.30 pm I fit in an emergency appointment. The patient is nine years old and has fallen off a wall. I clean him up and check how badly his teeth are damaged. He's frightened and calming him down is not easy.

4.30 pm A practice meeting. We talk about a possible move to bigger premises, which would mean employing more staff.

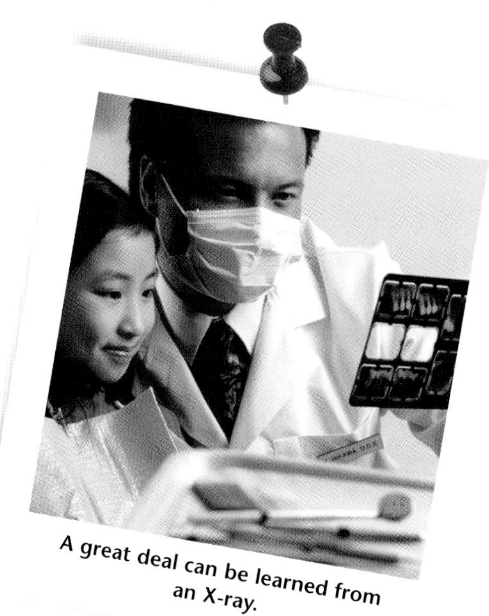

A great deal can be learned from an X-ray.

Doctor

What is a doctor?

Doctors diagnose (identify) illnesses, diseases and injuries. They decide on the right treatment for patients and follow their progress, to see if the treatment is a success. In some cases doctors treat patients themselves, in others they send them to a specialist who knows a great deal about a particular area of medicine.

An important part of a doctor's work is keeping patients healthy. They give advice on how to remain fit and well. This can include:

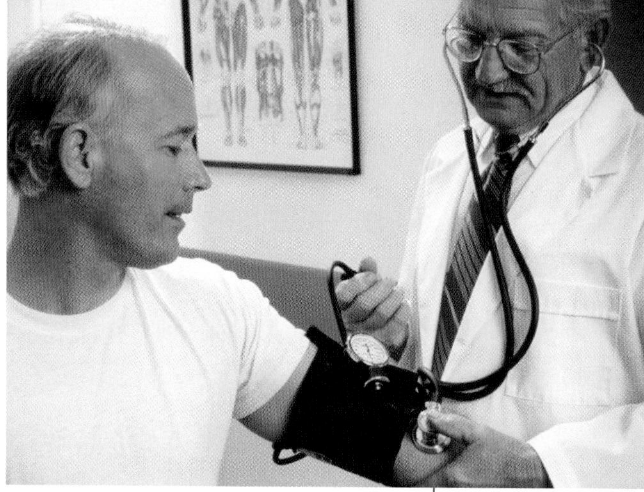

Regular health checks play an important part in keeping well.

- Running regular check-up sessions for healthy patients.
- Giving advice on matters such as:
  eating a healthy diet;
  losing weight;
  taking suitable exercise;
  giving up smoking;
  avoiding heart disease.

Doctors work as general practitioners (GPs) in the community, seeing patients for appointments in health centres and surgeries or visiting them at home.

Barber-surgeons

During the Middle Ages, people in need of surgery would visit a barber-surgeon. Barber-surgeons used razors to perform operations, cut hair and shave beards. They also pulled out teeth and set broken bones. Unlike doctors, they usually had no medical training at all.

Their shops attracted customers by a red and white striped pole outside which stood for blood and bandages. These poles can still be found outside some barbers' shops today.

They also work in hospitals and clinics where they usually specialize in a particular type of medicine.

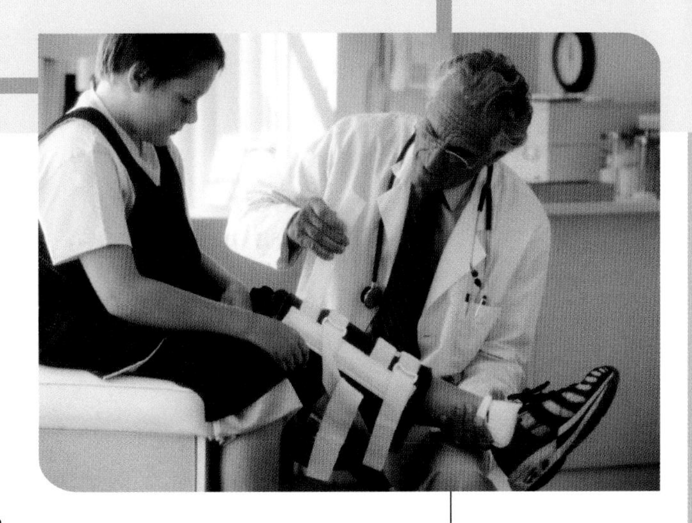

Some doctors specialize in treating a particular part of the body.

Some doctors work for the National Health Service, which provides free treatment. Some work in private practice, which means patients pay them for the treatment they give. Others work for both the NHS and in private practice. Many doctors are self-employed.

Main tasks of a doctor

The work done by doctors varies a great deal. General practitioners (GPs) are the first people patients visit with their medical problems. More and more doctors are choosing to specialize in different areas of medicine. There are over 60 medical specialisms, which fall into the following groups.

Medical specialities
These cover most of the conditions for which people go into hospital including:
accident and emergency;
cardiology (heart diseases);
oncology (cancers).

Surgical specialities
Carrying out operations on different parts of the body, such as:
the brain – neuro-surgery;
bones and joints – orthopaedic surgery.

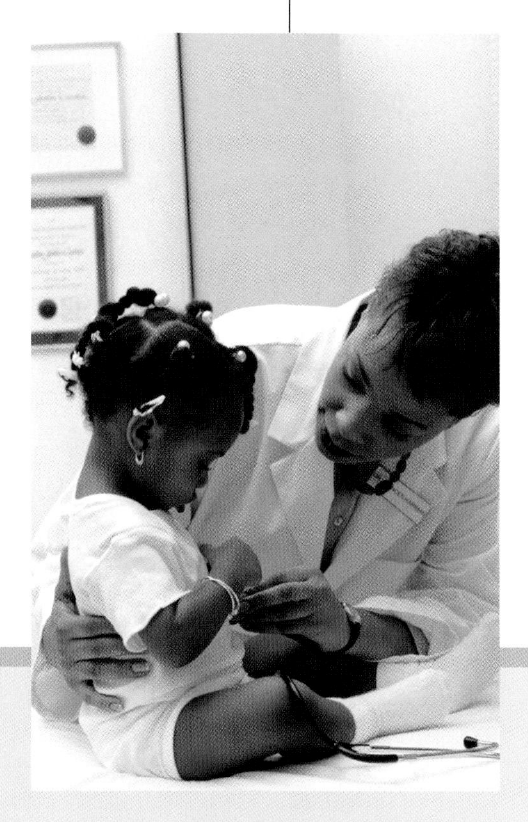

Paediatricians treat babies and children.

Good points and bad points

'I didn't consider specializing in anaesthetics, until I spent several months working in Africa, during my medical training and watched anaesthetists at work.'

'The training is long and tiring but to me it's worth it.'

Psychiatry
Psychiatrists work with patients suffering from mental illnesses or disabilities.

Paediatrics
Paediatricians treat babies and children with medical or developmental problems.

Obstetrics and gynaecology
Obstetricians and gynaecologists treat women's diseases. Most of their work has to do with pregnancy and childbirth.

Pathology
Pathologists investigate the causes and effects of diseases.

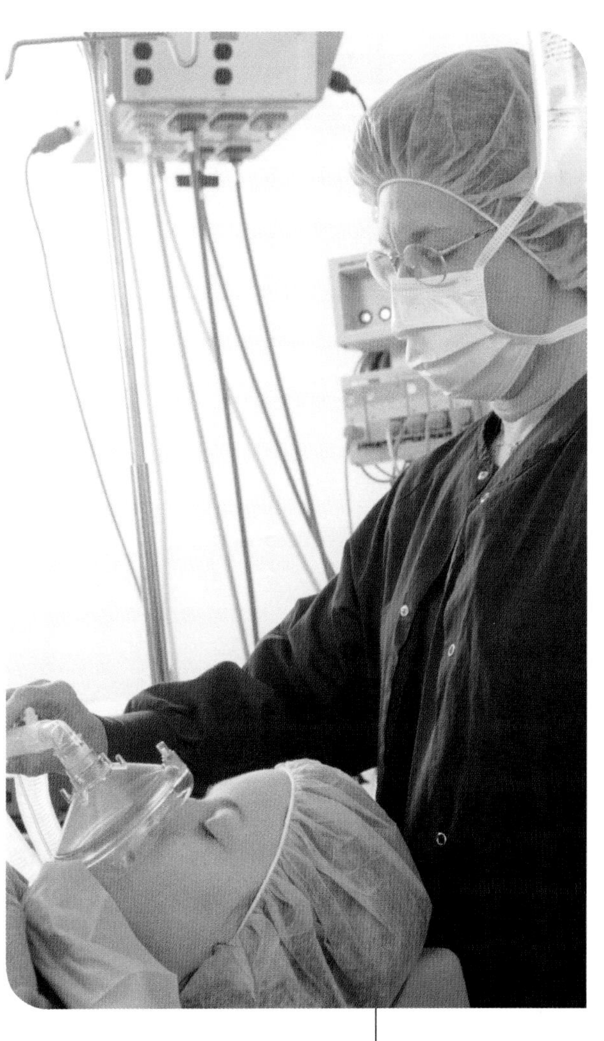

Anaesthetists make sure patients do not feel pain during surgery.

Radiology
Producing images of part of the body such as x-rays and scans to help diagnose disease and injuries. Also using radiation to treat illnesses such as cancer.

Anaesthetics
Anaesthetists administer and control the drugs and other substances required to put a patient to sleep during an operation or treatment.

Skills needed to be a doctor

High level of medical knowledge

Every area of medicine involves learning a great deal. The training is long and studies are at a high academic level. An important part of a doctor's work is examining a patient's symptoms, asking the right questions, carrying out tests and then working out what could be wrong. This can take a great deal of skill, knowledge and patience.

Commitment

Being a doctor may sound romantic. Television dramas often show good-looking doctors leading exciting lives. These do not give a true picture of a doctor's life. Most doctors work long hours and often come home very tired.

Friendly manner

Doctors need to comfort patients and their families. This is not easy when people are worried or frightened. Doctors also need to explain in ways people can understand, exactly what is wrong and how they will be treated.

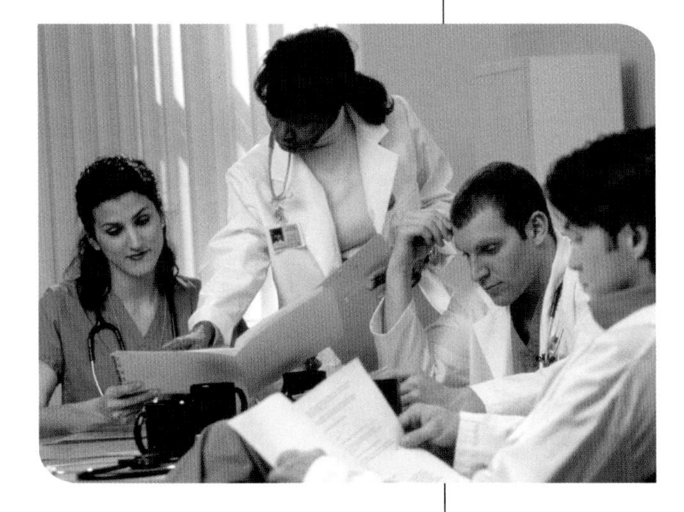

Doctors work as part of a team with other doctors, consultants and surgeons.

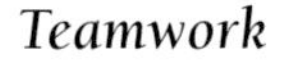

Teamwork

No doctor works alone. They form part of a team of health professionals including nurses, pharmacists and therapists. All these people work closely together to give patients the best possible treatment.

Medical students learn from qualified doctors.

fact file

It can take a very long time indeed to become a doctor. Students need 'A' Levels (including chemistry) before they will be accepted on the five-year degree course. It takes another four years to become a GP. Hospital **consultants** study and train for a total of around 12 years before they are qualified.

A strong stomach
Doctors deal with some very unpleasant sights and carry out some difficult tasks. They have to cope with the mess caused by injuries and operations including blood and vomit.

Emotional strength
No matter how hard doctors try, not all patients can be made well. Doctors have to accept this and move on to their next case positively.

A day in the life of a doctor

Jane Allen

Jane works as a junior doctor in the accident and emergency department of a busy hospital.

8.00 am I arrive for work. The department is always open, to treat people who have been injured or suddenly taken ill. Some arrive by ambulance and others in private cars.

During the night there have been two serious car accidents in the town and everyone is busy. Some patients are badly hurt and need to be admitted for treatment. Others need to be treated for minor injuries such as cuts and bruises.

We also have to talk to relatives of people involved in the accidents, who arrive looking for news.

11.00 am The department is quieter, but there are still patients to see.

12.00 pm The first sports injury arrives from a local rugby club. It's a young man with what looks like a broken collar bone. I arrange for X-rays so I can see exactly what is wrong.

1.45 pm I've managed a quick lunch and I'm back to see a woman on holiday in the area. She is expecting a baby and it has decided to arrive early. After examining her I arrange for her to go to the maternity ward.

3.30 pm I've now seen at least four more sports injuries. Keeping fit can be quite dangerous.

5.00 pm Guests from a wedding arrive. There are about six of them who've all drunk a great deal on a hot day and have collapsed. They need to be watched carefully until they recover.

5.30 pm Time for a short break before coming back to work for the evening.

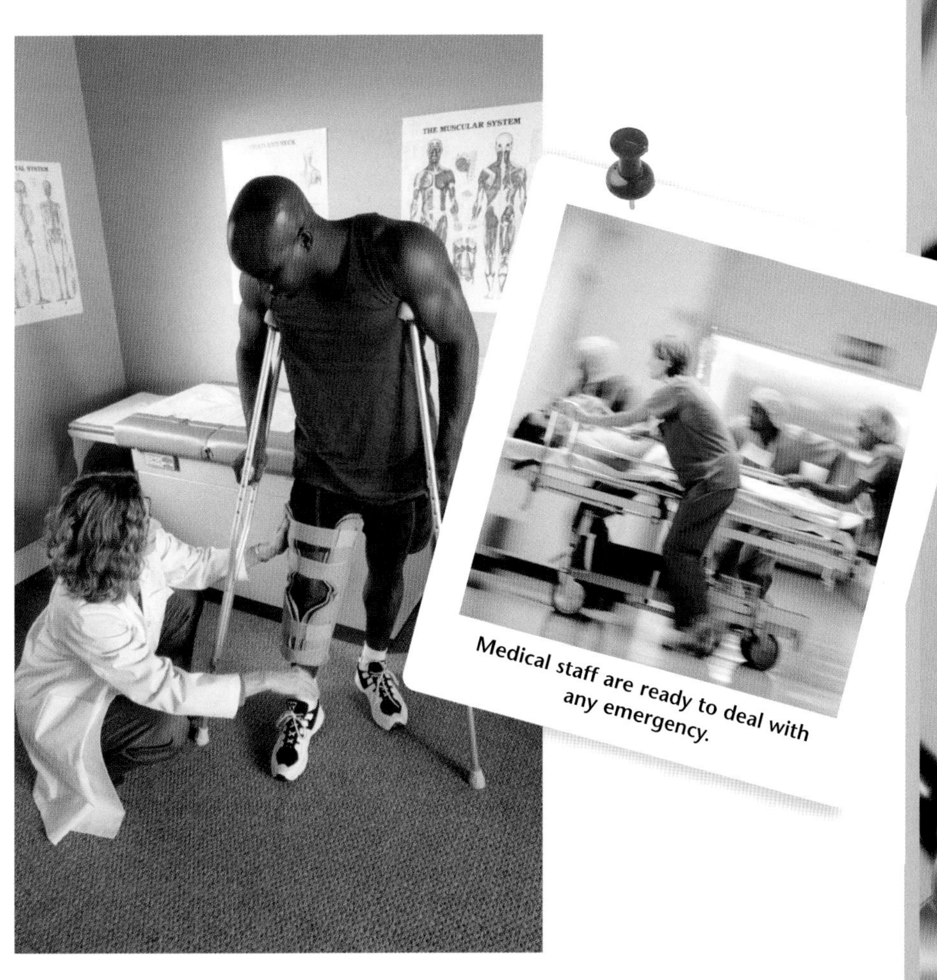

Medical staff are ready to deal with any emergency.

Some injuries need a lot of treatment.

Health Visitor

What is a health visitor?

Health visitors work in the community, visiting people in their own homes and helping those who are ill to recover and those who are fit to stay healthy.

They work with people of all ages from the newly born to the elderly and offer a wide range of support.

Health visitors travel to their patients' homes.

Health visitors work as part of a team attached to a medical practice, together with doctors, nurses and midwives. They also work closely with other people in the community such as teachers and social workers.

Although health visitors treat individual patients they also work with whole families. For instance if they visit a family with young children, they also check the children are well.

Helping hands

Health visitors come from many different working backgrounds. What is important is that they have the sympathy and practical skills to help other people.

This job involves giving comfort and support.

They take the time to chat with the parents and give them a chance to talk about any concerns they have.

In the same way health visitors going to see elderly people would encourage them to talk about whatever was worrying them.

As well as visiting people at home, health visitors run clinics and support groups in health centres, community centres and day centres.

Those working in rural areas often spend a lot of time on the road, driving from place to place.

Main tasks of a health visitor

Most health visitors are attached to a doctor's practice. They offer advice on a wide range of different subjects. Their main tasks include:

- Giving advice, information and support on how to stop smoking.
- Helping people to deal with the death of a member of their family or a close friend.
- Visiting people with long-term health problems or disabilities and putting them in touch with organizations which can help them.
- Encouraging elderly people to eat well and keep fit.
- Explaining about special safety and mobility equipment such as stair-rails.

Encouraging elderly patients to look after themselves is part of a health visitor's job.

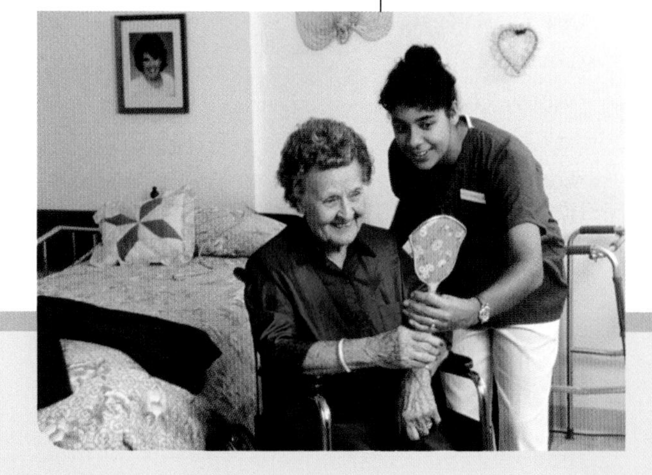

Good points and bad points

'I enjoy carrying out development checks in a family home. The atmosphere is relaxed and it's a chance to chat with parents or carers about any worries they have.

'Sometimes I find the amount of travelling I do is quite depressing especially when the weather is bad and I'm out in my car.'

Health visitors sometimes give people advice on how to eat well and stay fit and healthy.

Health visitors work very closely with families with young children. Their work includes:

- Giving advice, for example how to cope with babies who don't sleep or feed well.
- Carrying out tests on children to make sure that they are growing well and developing as they should, for example walking and talking at the right age.
- Running child immunization programmes to protect children against serious illnesses such as polio, measles and mumps.

Health visitors sometimes have to suggest tactfully to patients different ways of doing things to make their living conditions better. They may also bring in other professionals such as housing officials or social workers to help a family.

Skills needed to be a health visitor

Warm, friendly personality
Health visitors have to win patients' confidence so they can talk about what is worrying them.

Tact and patience
It takes time for people to talk about important matters and there is no point in trying to hurry them. When they are worried or unwell, patients can become rude or angry and health visitors have to deal with this.

Calm approach
Health visitors can walk into difficult situations, which they have to deal with quietly and sensibly.

A health visitor must always be calm, friendly and reassuring.

Speaking skills
When talking to patients, health visitors need to explain complicated situations simply and answer questions in a clear way.

Written skills
They have to write reports and letters which are clear and easily understood.

Understanding
Health visitors can see some distressing situations and they need to be able to help people involved in them. This means accepting them and not blaming them for what has happened, or the way in which they are living.

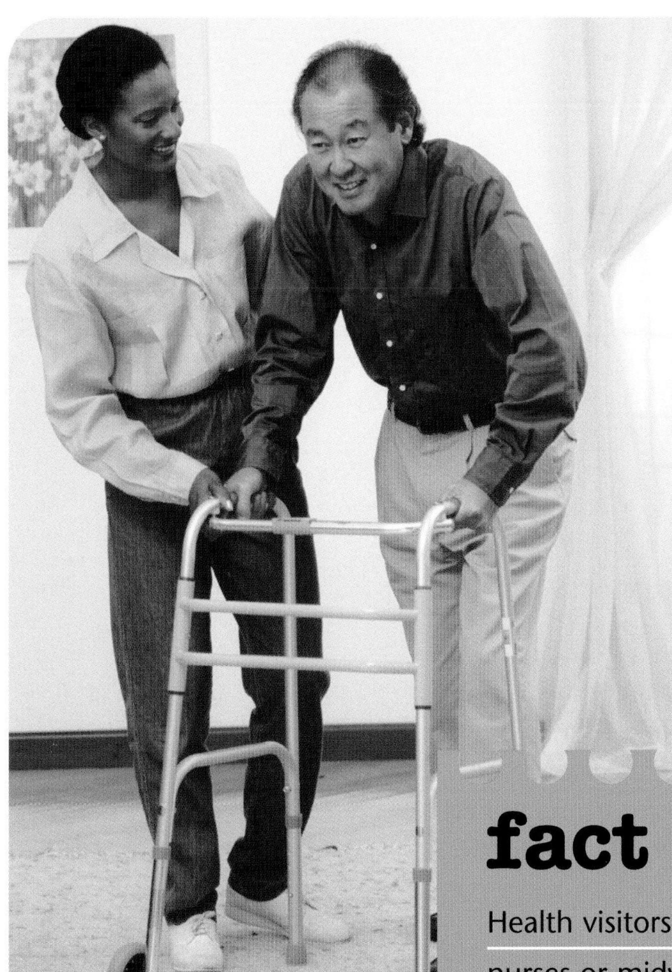

It can take time to recover from an accident or illness.

fact file

Health visitors are qualified nurses or midwives who have taken further training to become a health visitor.

Good organizational skills
Health visitors are often in charge of planning their own day, working out a timetable for visiting patients and running clinics. To do this well they have to be able to plan ahead and make the best use of their time.

A day in the life of a health visitor

Martha Brown

Martha works as a health visitor in a large city.

8.45 am I call into the medical centre to check for any urgent messages. I have three new babies to visit this morning. I carry a map in my car in case I get lost.

9.15 am The first parents already have a three-year-old and seem relaxed with their new baby. I stay for a chat, take a look at the baby and explain to the parents how I can be contacted if there is a problem.

10.30am I'm concerned about my next mother because she has a large family and she's been unwell. We talk about a nursery place for two of the children, which she thinks would be a good idea. I'm going to find out some more information and come back in a few days.

12.30 pm The third baby is restless and his parents are exhausted. They both feel they're not very good parents. I tell them most people go through times of feeling like this.

Without a health visitor, many people would have to move to a retirement home.

Patients are often on medication prescribed by their doctors. Health visitors check that patients are taking it regularly.

2.00 pm It's time for a baby clinic when parents and carers bring children in for developmental tests and immunizations and talk over any worries. There's also a chance for people to get together for a chat and listen to a talk. Today it's on baby massage and the adults seem to enjoy it as much as the babies.

5.00 pm I check my diary. Tomorrow I have some elderly patients to visit and a meeting with the rest of the medical team to talk over extra help needed by some of our patients.

Mental Health Worker

What is a mental-health worker?

Mental-health workers work with patients who have mental-health problems, but do not have to stay in hospital.

Many people suffer from **anxiety** or **depression** at some time in their lives. While some are able to cope and soon begin to feel better, others need help before they start to recover.

In the past, people with mental-health problems were sent to large hospitals to be treated. Sometimes, they stayed there for so long that they became unable to manage life outside.

Mental-health workers help people to cope with mental-health problems.

Coming to terms with the problem

Most people find it easier to talk about illnesses in their bodies (physical illnesses) than illnesses in their minds (mental illnesses).

However, one in six people suffers from a mental illness at some time in their life. This means that mental-health problems are as common as asthma.

When patients return from a stay in hospital, mental-health workers help them to settle back into life at home.

Things are very different today. Although some people do need to be admitted to hospital with mental-health disorders, many more live in the community. Mental-health workers support those who live in their own homes or in **sheltered accommodation**, helping them to live life to the full.

Some mental-health workers are based in medical centres, working as part of a medical team. Some run **day centres** for patients who live at home. Others work in residential hostels where groups of patients live together with trained staff.

They also work in drug- or alcohol-dependency units, which help people who have problems linked to drug or alcohol use.

Main tasks of a mental-health worker

Mental-health workers help those with a wide range of mental-health problems to live as normal a life as possible. Some problems they deal with include: depression and anxiety; eating disorders, such as **anorexia** and **bulimia**; and drug or alcohol abuse. The work of mental-health workers includes:

- Monitoring patients' medication – making sure that they are taking their medicine in the right amounts and at the right time.

- Noticing changes – both big and small – in the way a patient behaves. These could show that the patient is getting better or becoming less well.

Mental-health workers organize therapy sessions for patients.

Good points and bad points

'Today, many people who would once have spent their lives in hospital are able to live in their own homes, make friends and even hold down jobs. I'm proud to think that I have made a difference.'

'Working in mental health is tiring. Patients can be nervous and upset and it can be difficult to win their trust.'

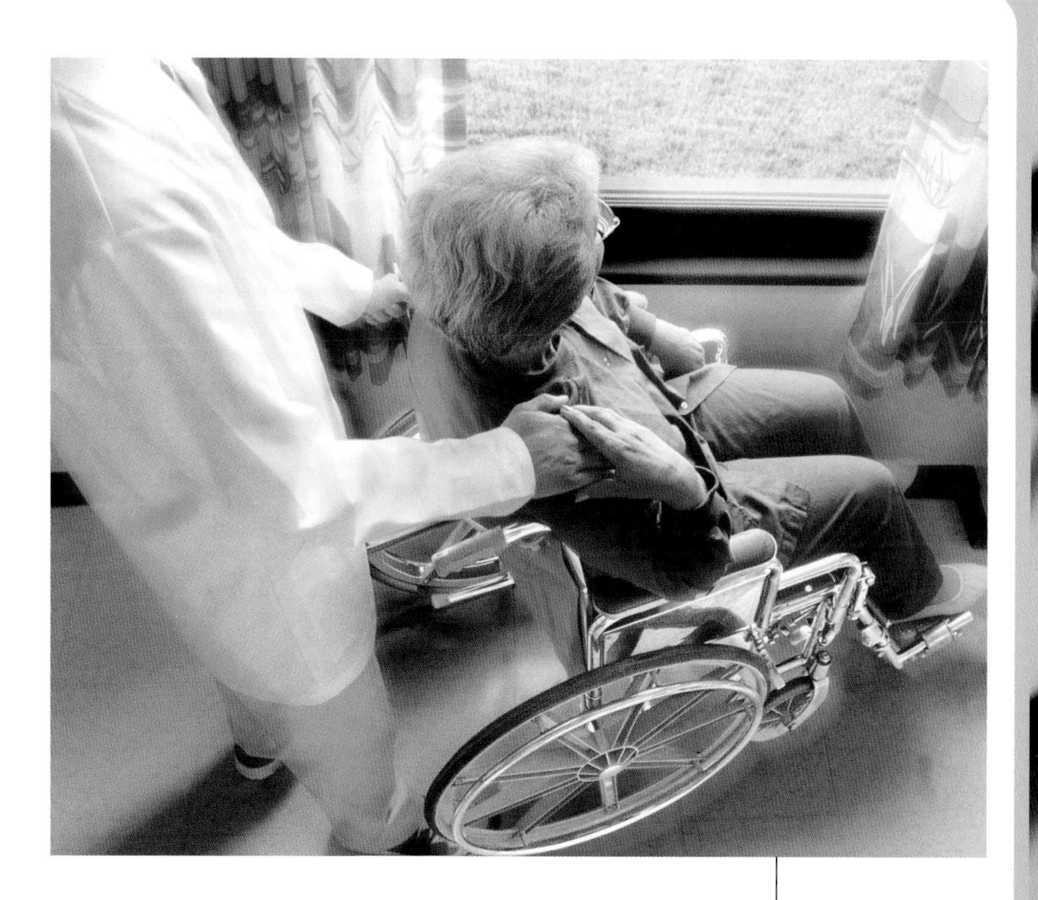

With help, many people are able to live in their own homes or in sheltered accommodation.

- Forming good relationships with patients and helping them to build the confidence they need to live full, interesting lives.
- Providing different sorts of therapy or treatment. This might involve counselling – talking over problems and their causes, either with a single patient or in small groups. Activity sessions of art, music or drama encourage patients to express how they feel.
- Helping families and friends of patients. Many people are ashamed of mental illness and need help to understand what is happening and how they can help.

Skills needed to be a mental-health worker

Calm, friendly approach
People with mental-health problems are not always easy to help. They can be nervous and angry, or quiet and withdrawn. Mental-health workers have to win patients' confidence before they can begin to help them.

Patience
Treatment cannot be hurried – progress is often very slow. Mental-health workers have to remain positive and continue encouraging patients to get well, even if they have suffered ill health for many years.

Meetings are held to discuss a patient's progress.

Good observational skills
Restlessness or tiredness in a patient, or other small signs, can give an early warning of problems. Mental-health workers need to be aware of such changes, so patients can be helped before matters become serious.

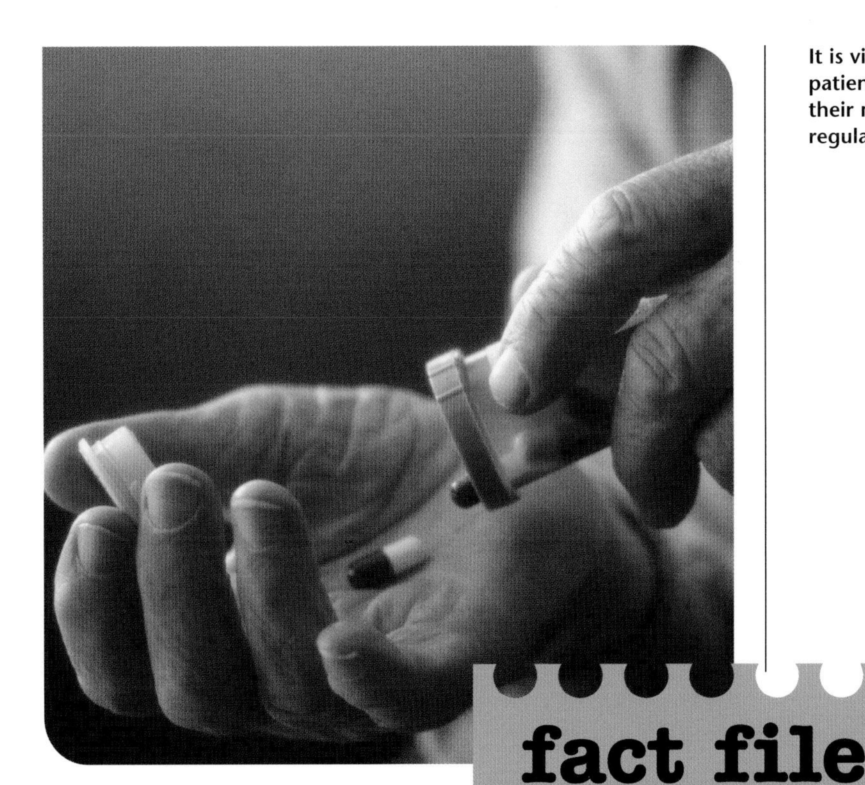

It is vital that patients take their medication regularly.

fact file

Mental-health workers take a diploma or a degree in nursing. This is followed by further study and supervised training in psychiatric work.

A calm head

People with mental-health problems can suffer from **mood swings**. They may be content one minute and upset the next. Mental-health workers need to be able to deal with difficult situations quietly and quickly, helping the patient to settle down again.

Team skills

A good support network is the best way to help people with mental-health problems. Mental-health workers form part of a team, working closely with doctors, **social workers** and **therapists**.

A day in the life of a mental-health worker

Frank Jeffs

Frank is a mental-health worker attached to a medical practice.

8.30 am There is a team meeting, when we all get together to talk over matters that are concerning us.

10.00 am I visit one of my patients. She has stayed in hospital for long stretches, but sometimes manages well at home. Her husband and daughter are there – we all talk about the patient's medication. I suggest that she comes to a day centre regularly to meet people and talk to staff.

11.00 am I arrive at the day centre. One young man is agitated, so I take him aside to calm him. (Part of my training included dealing with this type of situation.) The patient is finding it difficult to remember to take his medication and also finds the company of other people upsetting. After our talk, the patient agrees that I should contact his **psychiatrist**. Together, we will come up with some ideas on how he can be helped.

12.30 pm The psychiatrist's secretary phones me to arrange a time for us to talk.

1.30 pm I spend some time chatting to the other patients at the day centre.

3.00 pm After a telephone conversation with the psychiatrist, I suggest to the patient that he has daily visits from the community psychiatric nursing team for the next few days. This will be followed by a visit to the psychiatrist.

4.30 pm I return to the medical centre to write up notes and reports of the day's events for my colleagues.

5.30 pm Time to go home.

Mental-health workers learn how to talk to patients in order to comfort, reassure or reason with them.

Mental-health workers help patients and their families to enjoy life again.

Nurse

What is a nurse?

Nurses care for people who are sick, injured or disabled. They also teach people about the importance of keeping fit and well.

As well as working in hospitals, nurses work in health centres, rehabilitation centres (where people recover from long-term illnesses or health problems), nursing homes, specialist clinics, the armed forces, prisons and schools. They also work in the community, looking after people in their own homes.

There are different branches of nursing. Nurses can choose to work with children, with adults or in mental-health nursing. Those who work in hospitals can specialize in a particular area of work, such as:

- Cancer care – looking after patients suffering from cancer.
- Theatre and recovery – caring for patients during operations and immediately afterwards.

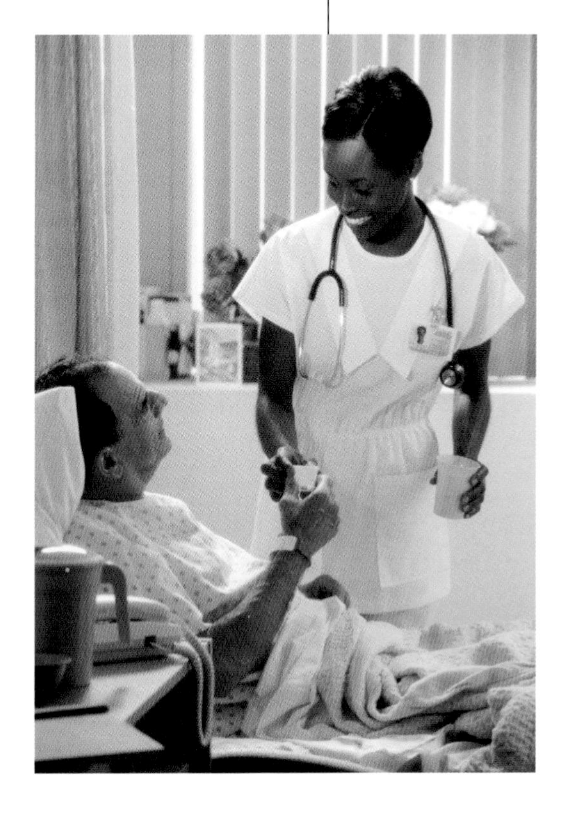

Nurses work in hospitals, nursing homes and hospices.

The lady of the lamp

In 1854, Florence Nightingale took a group of nurses to Scutari, in Turkey. There, they looked after wounded soldiers from the Crimean War. Florence used to walk around the wards at night, checking on her patients by the light of her lamp. She became known as the Lady of the Lamp. Florence later realized that the dirty conditions in which the soldiers were nursed had caused many deaths. She introduced strict rules of cleanliness and hygiene, which saved many lives.

Some nurses treat sick people in their own homes.

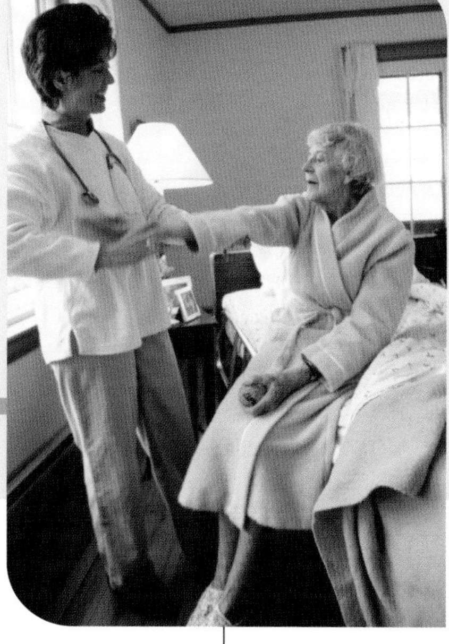

- Intensive care – looking after very sick people who need a great deal of attention.
- Accident and emergency – caring for people who have just arrived at the hospital. Accident and emergency staff decide what happens to these patients – whether they are treated on the spot or whether they are sent to different wards for treatment.

Nurses, especially those who work in hospitals, often need to work irregular and unsociable hours, including nights and weekends.

Main tasks of a nurse

Nurses work with a team of professionals including doctors, **dieticians**, **physiotherapists** and **radiographers**. They form close relationships with patients, getting to know them, giving them reassurance and answering their questions.

All nurses look after the sick, but there are some differences in the jobs performed by those working in hospitals and those in the community.

Hospital nurses:

- Collect and record information about their patients regularly – this can involve checking temperatures and measuring blood-pressure levels.
- Clean and dress wounds – if wounds are not kept clean, they can become infected and patients can die.

Nurses work in **operating theatres** supporting surgeons.

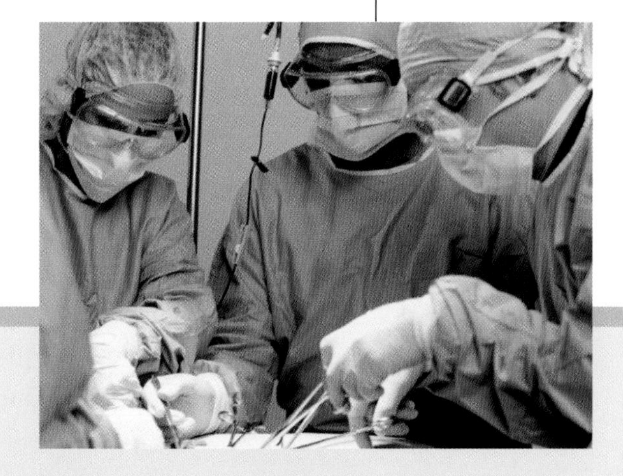

Good points and bad points

'No two days are ever the same in nursing – and that's what I like. The unexpected is always happening.'

'The work is hard. It can be upsetting when patients don't get better, despite our efforts.'

- Give patients medication – nurses are responsible for making sure that patients receive the right medication at the right time. They also give patients injections.
- Assist doctors in the operating theatre by: checking on the health of the patient during the operation; setting out all the necessary instruments, and handing these instruments to surgeons as needed.

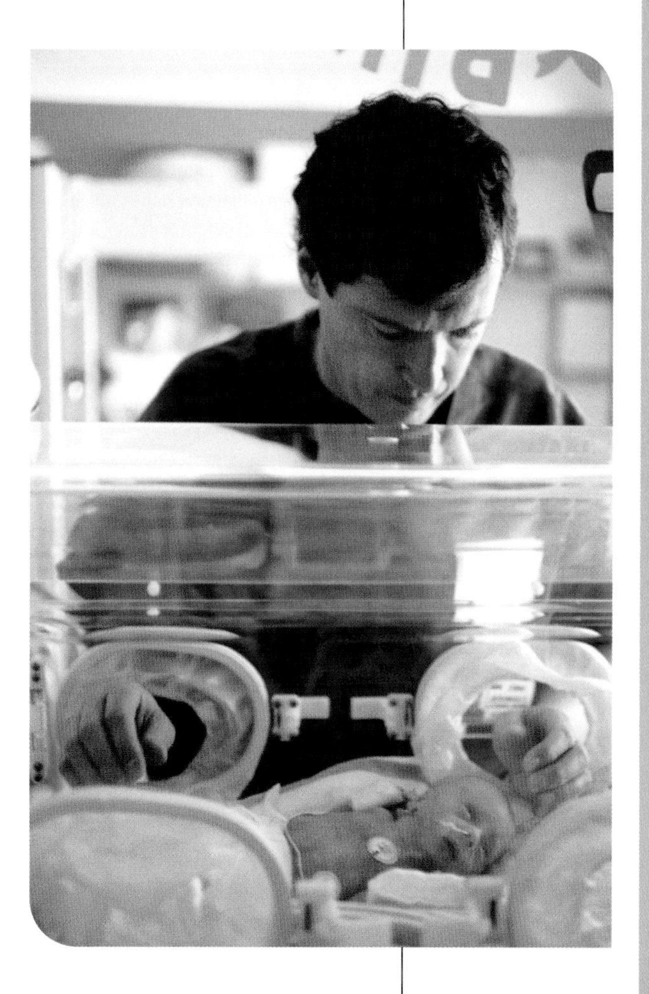

Nurses can choose to specialize in looking after premature babies.

Community nurses:

- Visit people whose condition needs to be regularly checked and those that are in need of medical support. This includes: the elderly, the disabled and those who have recently returned home after hospital treatment.

They also:

- change dressings and bandages;
- take blood samples for testing;
- give medication;
- check patients' progress;
- support patients' families.

Skills needed to be a nurse

Knowledge
Nurses need special training to learn all about the human body and how it works. They also need to know how to look after people.

Attention to detail
Nurses must make sure that every part of their work is done exactly as it should be. Any change in a patient, even a very slight one, must be noted down or passed on to colleagues.

A gentle touch
When cleaning wounds, removing dressings or taking out stitches, nurses need to work with great care, so a patient is hurt as little as possible.

A friendly approach
Being ill or injured can be a frightening experience. Nurses need to help patients to talk about their worries, so they can reassure them.

Before going off-duty, nurses brief the new team on patients' progress.

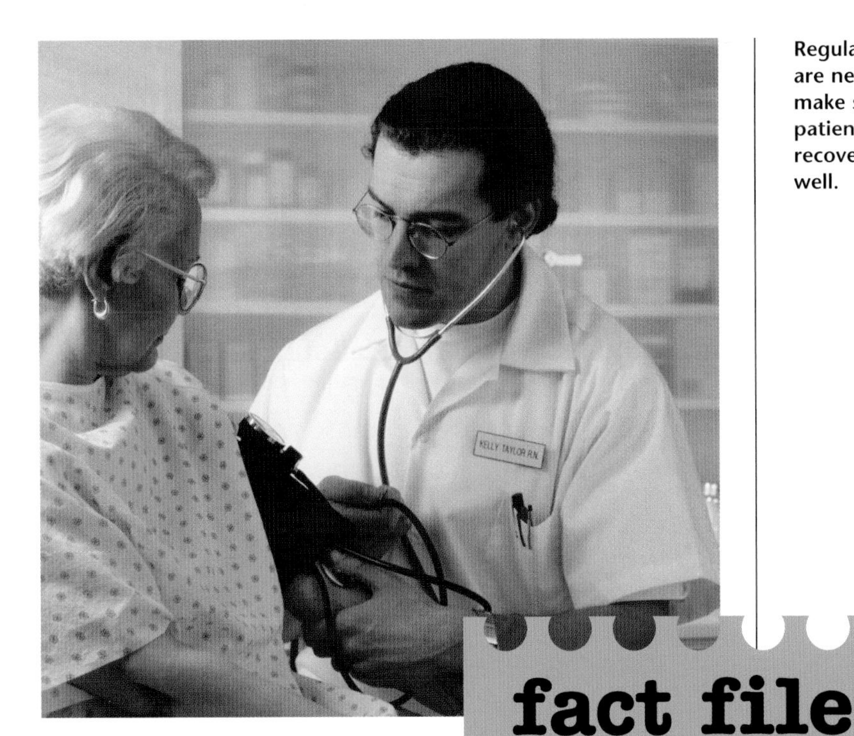

Regular checks are needed to make sure a patient is recovering well.

fact file

To be a nurse you need to complete a **degree** or **diploma** course. This includes coursework and practical experience working with patients, while being supervised by experienced staff.

Communication skills
Patients need to know what is wrong with them and what treatment they will be given. Nurses have to explain matters to patients in a straightforward way, so that they can understand what is happening.

Good written skills
Details of patients' progress and the treatment they are receiving are recorded on charts and in reports. These have to be clear, so there are no misunderstandings.

A strong stomach
Nurses have to deal with blood, vomit and mess.

John Whittaker

John is a nurse on a critical-care ward (intensive care). At the moment, he is working nights, so most of his day is spent sleeping. During the week, he works two long shifts and two shorter ones. Today, he's working a long shift.

6.00 pm I get up, shower and make myself something to eat. Then I watch television for a while before setting off for hospital.

9.00 pm Together with the rest of the night team, I'm briefed by the staff who are finishing their shift.

All the patients on the critical-care ward need a great deal of attention. The handover process is the time to listen and ask questions. We need to make sure that we're prepared for anything that might happen during the night.

10.00 pm We spend our time checking patients and making sure that they are comfortable.

1.00 am I check a middle-aged man who came in this morning following a heart attack. I notice that his pulse and breathing are becoming faster, and within a few seconds the cardiac monitor is showing that the patient is suffering heart failure.

A doctor is soon on the scene to treat the patient. Because the heart failure was detected early, he will almost certainly make a good recovery.

3.00 am I take a late break. Somehow, I never feel like eating at this time of the night.

4.00 am Back on the ward, I carry on with my rounds, dealing with phone calls about the possible transfer of a patient who is currently in the accident and emergency department.

6.00 am It's getting lighter outside – time to think about the coming handover. We all need to be there to answer questions about particular patients.

8.30 am Everyone else is getting up. Soon, I'll be in bed.

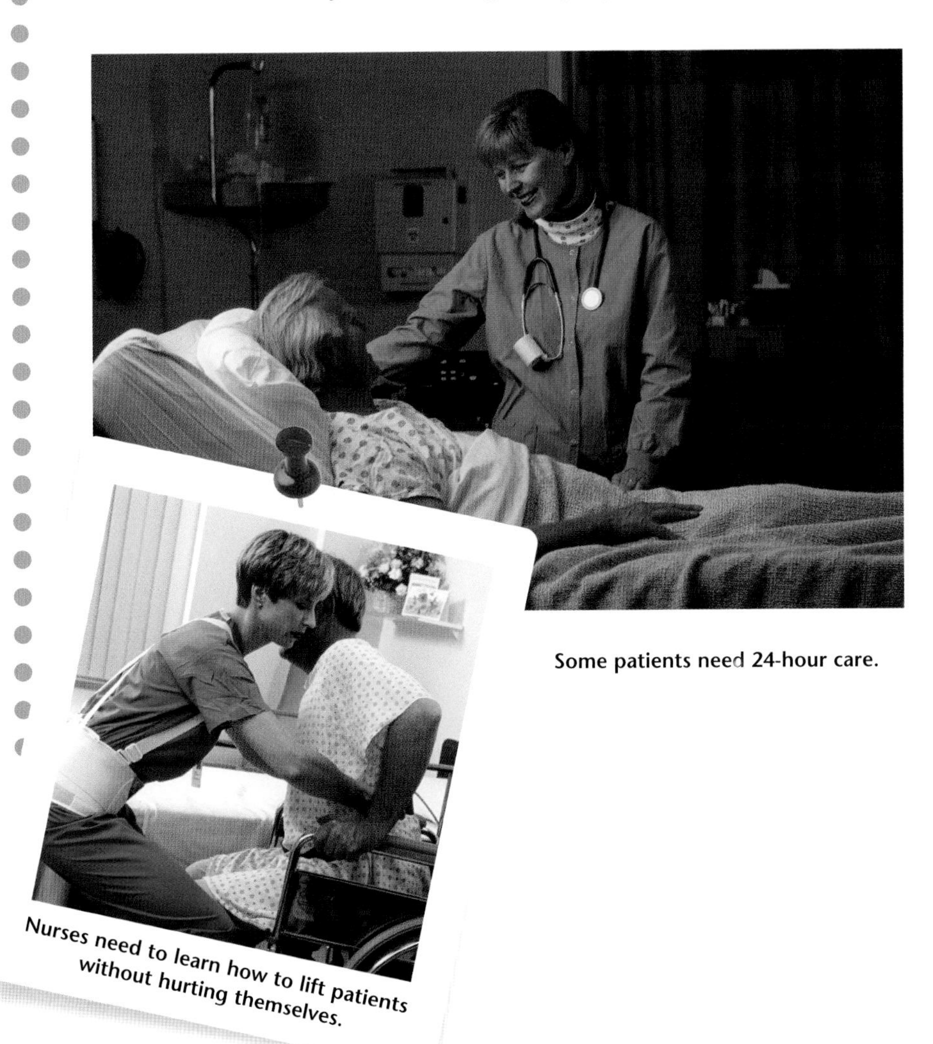

Some patients need 24-hour care.

Nurses need to learn how to lift patients without hurting themselves.

Optician

What is an optician?

Opticians – also known as optometrists – look after and treat sight problems. Not everybody has perfect vision. Even those who have good eyesight when they are young may need to wear glasses as they grow older. Some children wear glasses for a short time, often to correct a squint or a lazy eye. Other people wear them throughout their lives.

Some people do not realize they have sight problems until it becomes difficult to read small print.

Who invented glasses?

Glasses, or spectacles, have been made for hundreds of years, but no one knows exactly when they were invented – or who invented them. The first glasses may have been made in Italy during the thirteenth century. However, they may have been invented in China at around the same time. Early glasses were balanced on the bridge of the nose – arms were not added until the seventeenth century.

A child might need to wear glasses for a short time to correct a problem.

Today, many people wear contact lenses instead of glasses. Contact lenses are small pieces of plastic that fit against the eye. Laser treatment is also becoming popular – this corrects vision permanently and can be carried out under a local anaesthetic.

Opticians examine eyes, test patients' sight and prescribe treatment, such as glasses or contact lenses. They also give advice to patients on the type of glasses that would suit them. Then, they order the glasses and make sure that they fit properly.

Main tasks of an optician

Opticians carry out eye tests to find out the strength and type of **lenses** needed to correct faulty vision.

They use special instruments to look at the inside of the eye. This means that they can check that eyes are healthy.

Patients suffering from eye problems that are caused by **diabetes**, **anaemia** or other illnesses are sent to opticians by their doctors.

Opticians refer patients to consultants if they suspect that there is a serious problem, such as:

- Glaucoma – damage to the **optic nerve** caused by fluid pressing on the inside of the eye.

It is possible to look into a patient's eye using an instrument called an **ophthalmoscope**.

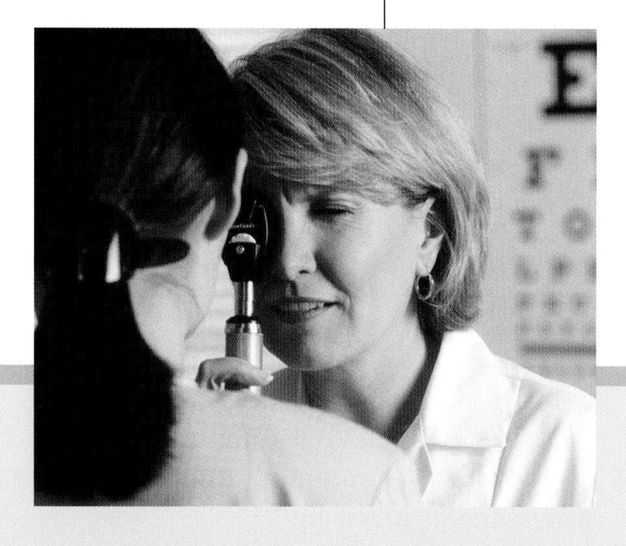

Good points and bad points

'Patients are delighted when new lenses improve their vision and they are able to enjoy reading and watching television once again.

'I see quite a lot of children. When I explain to them what I am doing, they usually remain calm. Occasionally a child does become frightened – this is distressing for everyone.'

- Detached retina – when the inner lining at the back of the eyeball becomes loose.
- Cataract – a condition that makes the lens dull instead of transparent, causing blurred vision.

It is important to choose the right frames. They need to feel comfortable and look smart.

Opticians help their patients to choose frames, then take measurements to make sure the glasses will fit properly. If the patient prefers contact lenses, opticians will tell them which types are suitable for their eyes.

When the glasses or contact lenses are ready they are usually ordered from a manufacturing company. Opticians check them against the original prescription. Then they fit the glasses or lenses, making sure that they improve patients' sight and are comfortable. They also give advice on how to care for them.

Skills needed to be an optician

Scientific knowledge

Opticians need to understand and recognize eye defects and know how to correct them. They also need to know how the whole body works. This is because some eye conditions are linked to conditions such as diabetes, anaemia or **brain tumours**.

A gentle touch

The eyes are very sensitive. Anyone dealing with them needs to have a gentle, accurate touch.

Communication skills

Explanations need to be clear and simple because many patients do not understand the meaning of scientific or medical words.

Friendly manner

Patients have to remain still while their eyes are being examined and must concentrate during an eye test. It is the optician's job to put them at their ease.

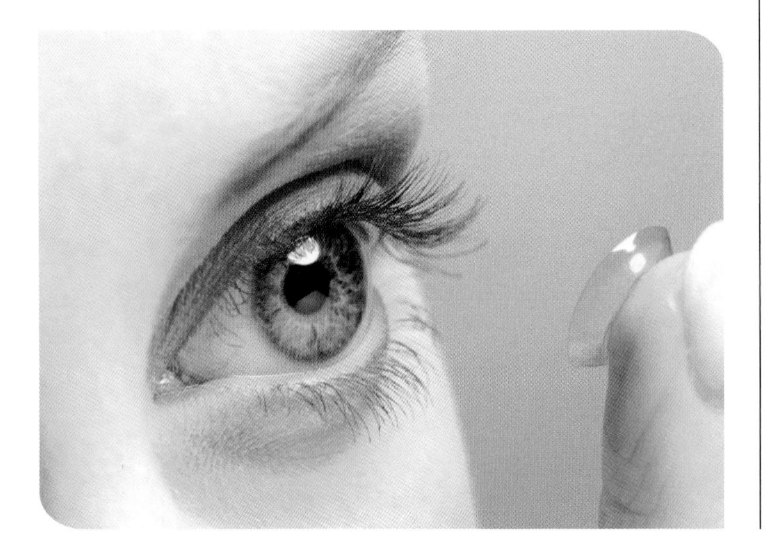

Many people wear contact lenses to improve their vision. Some wear them to change the colour of their eyes.

Many famous designers create their own stylish frames.

fact file

Ophthalmic opticians take a three-year degree course, then spend a further year training – this involves practical experience. They qualify after taking a final exam.

Business skills

Many opticians are self-employed. This means keeping detailed records of sales and expenses and taking the necessary decisions to keep the business profitable.

An eye for trends

Fashions in glasses are always changing. Opticians need to know about the latest styles, so that they can sell them to patients.

A day in the life of an optician

Lauren Burgess

Lauren is an optician working in a large practice with seven other opticians. They are based in modern premises in a shopping precinct. The receptionist makes their appointments.

9.00 am My first patient has worn glasses ever since she was a teenager. She has regular check-ups for any changes in her vision. This time, the lenses of her glasses don't need changing. However she would like new frames, so I refer her to one of the dispensing opticians.

10.30 am A new patient arrives. Recently, he has found it increasingly difficult to read newsprint. I ask him questions about his general health and suggest that he talks over some of his symptoms with his doctor.

2.00 pm I see a teenager who would like contact lenses because she feels embarrassed wearing glasses. After testing the patient's eyes, I talk to her and her mother, who is worried about the cost and the difficulties of putting in lenses. I explain about the different possibilities and suggest they come back when they've decided how they'd like to proceed.

3.30 pm I spend time with the receptionist, who is also the practice secretary. I'd like her to type some letters for me. We check over my appointments – I ask her to keep some dates free next month, so I can attend a conference. It's important to keep up with all the new developments in eye treatment and care.

4.30 pm My last patient of the day arrives – she has come for an eye test after finishing work.

Letter charts form one part of the eye test.

Glasses come in all shapes and sizes.

Pharmacist

What is a pharmacist?

Pharmacists are experts in the use of medicine and drugs. They make up medicines and dispense them to people, with instructions on how and when they should be taken. They also offer advice on pain relief and on treatments for minor **ailments** such as **indigestion**, allergies, coughs and colds.

In the past, people relied solely on herbs to heal injuries and treat illness.

Apothecaries

Early pharmacists – known as apothecaries – had little training or medical knowledge. Most would have had some understanding of **botany**, chemistry and medicine. They used this knowledge to make medicines, which they sold to people to cure their illnesses. Medicines were often made from the plants and herbs that apothecaries grew in their gardens. While some treatments were helpful, many were no use at all.

Modern pharmacists deal with a wide range of drugs and medicines.

All pharmacies where drugs are sold must be under the direct control of a qualified and registered pharmacist. Most pharmacists work in the community, in retail shops and dispensaries. Some are self-employed and run their own pharmacy businesses.

Pharmacists also work in hospital pharmacies, purchasing and testing hospital medicines and dispensing them to different wards and departments.

Not all pharmacists work in healthcare. Some work for **pharmaceutical companies** with other scientists, developing and testing new drugs.

Main tasks of a pharmacist

Community pharmacists

Customers bring pharmacists their **prescriptions**. These are instructions written by a doctor – they tell the pharmacist the medicine or drug that the patient requires and the amount to be given to them.

Pharmacists validate prescriptions. This means they check the information and, if they have any concerns about it, they contact the doctor who wrote the prescription. If everything is in order, pharmacists make up the prescriptions and dispense them to customers.

Pharmacists also advise customers on symptoms and general health matters, such as healthy eating and the best ways to stop smoking. They also sell medicines that do not require a prescription directly to customers.

A pharmacist must make sure the patient is given the correct amount of a drug.

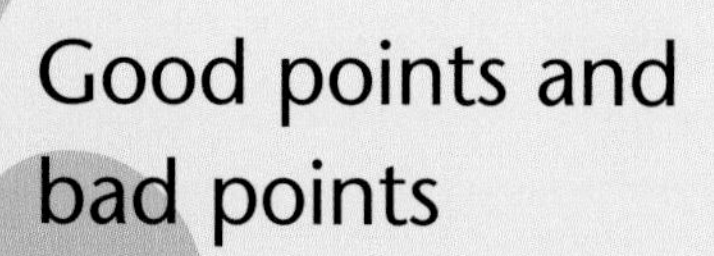

Good points and bad points

'I work in a large pharmacy and meet a lot of people as part of my job. I feel that we offer a good service to people.'

'At times we are very busy. However, we always have to make sure that everything is checked and double-checked so everybody receives the right medication. There's no room for error.'

Customers often want to chat to their local pharmacist.

It is the pharmacist's responsibility to make sure that all medicines are stored safely. It is important that they do not get into the wrong hands. They keep up-to-date, detailed records listing drugs that they have in stock and those that have been sold.

Hospital pharmacists

The work of hospital pharmacists is similar to that of community pharmacists. However, in a hospital, pharmacists work as part of the medical team, advising staff on the best medication for individual patients and the amount that should be prescribed.

Skills needed to be a pharmacist

A high level of scientific knowledge
Pharmacists train for many years. They have to know a great deal about different substances and their effect upon the human body.

A calm, reassuring manner
Customers may be worried about their own health or that of their family. They look for positive advice from a pharmacist on matters such as smoking and weight loss. Pharmacists also need to check with customers that they know how to take their medication and that they understand about any side effects. For example, some drugs have to be taken immediately after food to avoid an upset stomach.

Responsibility
Every day, pharmacists deal with dangerous drugs. They must make sure that they and their staff follow strict safety guidelines. The pharmacy, whether in a hospital or in a store, must be secure at all times, to make sure that the substances kept there cannot be illegally removed.

Eye for detail
Even when they are working quickly and are under pressure to make up prescriptions, pharmacists need to check them carefully. They must make sure that the medications prescribed will not react against each other and that the amounts prescribed are correct.

In a pharmacy, careful checks need to be made.

Computer skills are vital for today's pharmacist.

fact file

Pharmacists take a four-year degree course, followed by a year's training in a pharmacy practice. State-registered pharmacists, who work in the NHS, also need to take another exam before they are qualified.

IT skills
Computers play an important part in record keeping. Staff should be able to use them with confidence.

Business skills
Self-employed pharmacists must be well organized with good commercial awareness in order to make a profit.

A day in the life of a pharmacist

Patsy McGee

Patsy is a newly qualified pharmacist working in a busy teaching hospital.

9.00 am I work in the hospital dispensary, where we make up prescriptions and send out medication. I have to check prescriptions, making sure that a patient is not given medicines that could react against each other. Once I've checked each prescription, I pass them on to a hospital pharmacy technician who dispenses them.

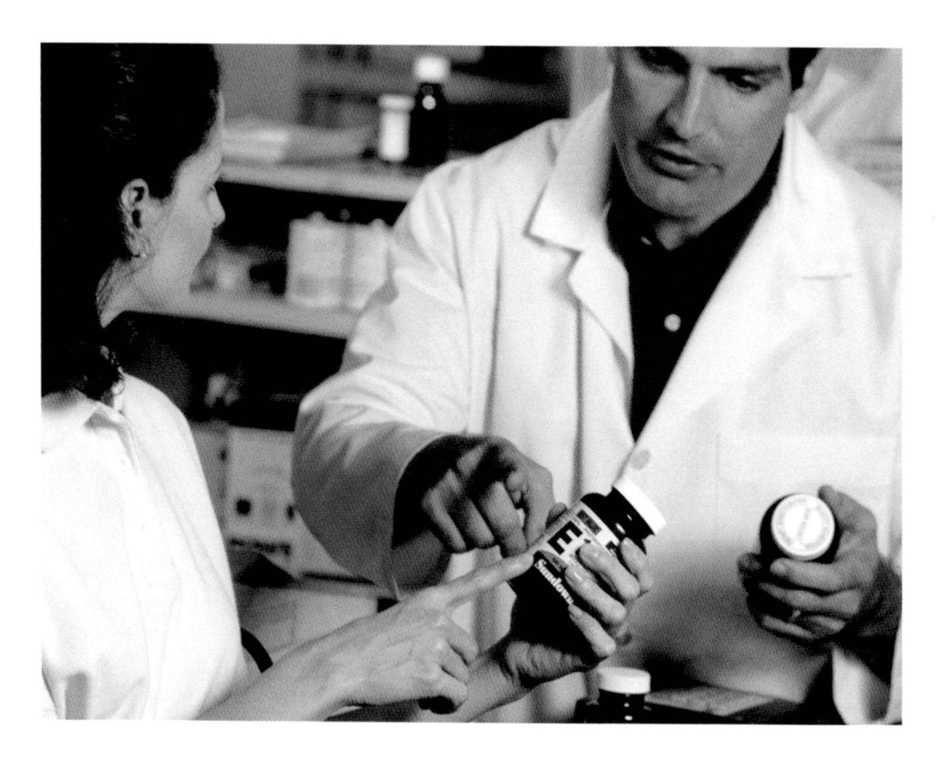

Pharmacists have lots of contact with patients.

11.30 am A patient who has been admitted to hospital is taking a drug we don't keep, so I contact the doctor to explain the problem and to suggest an alternative.

12.30 pm At lunchtime, I usually eat in the hospital canteen.

2.00 pm I am responsible for two wards. In the afternoon I visit them, checking each patient's drug chart. I look at their notes to gain more information and speak to doctors, nurses and the patients themselves. Then I make any suggestions I can to improve treatment.

5.00 pm I talk to a patient who is finding it difficult swallowing a high dose of **morphine**. I suggest to the doctor that we might use patches instead, so the drug is released through the skin.

Pharmacists must check prescriptions before validating them.

Glossary

agencies – organizations which look after a particular area of healthcare in the community.

anaemia – a condition of the blood where there are not enough red blood cells and the patient looks pale and feels exhausted.

anaesthetics – drugs given to patients to make them unconscious before an operation.

anorexia – an illness where people believe they are overweight and refuse to eat.

anxiety – worry.

appointments – a set time given to see a professional person such as a doctor.

ailments – illnesses.

botany – the study of flowers and plants.

brain tumour – a growth or swelling on the brain.

bulimia – an illness where people believe they are overweight and make themselves sick after meals.

cap – a piece of material used to build up a broken tooth.

consultants - medical specialists.

crown – a false tooth fitted over a damaged or decayed tooth.

day centres – places where people go to meet others, take part in different activities and have a meal.

decay – rotting.

degree – a certificate given when a university course has been completed.

dentures – false teeth.

depression – an illness which causes people to feel miserable and unhappy for long periods of time.

diabetes – an illness caused when people cannot control the level of sugar in their blood.

dieticians – people who are trained to give advice to people about what they eat.

diploma – certificate to show someone has completed a training or learning course.

dispense – make up medicines from doctors' prescriptions.

filling – material put in a tooth to replace a decaying section.

general practitioners – doctors who work in the community treating patients with a wide range of problems.

heart disease – illness or condition affecting the heart, making it difficult for it to work properly.

hygienists – dental staff who clean and scale patients' teeth.

intensive care – nursing of patients who are very ill and need a lot of attention.

laboratories – places containing scientific equipment where tests and experiments are carried out.

lenses – pieces of curved glass, used to correct eyesight.

medication – drugs, ointments, or mixtures of different substances prescribed by a doctor for a patient.

mood swings – feeling happy one minute and then suddenly feeling depressed.

morphine – a pain-killing drug.

operating theatres – rooms where surgeons operate on anaesthetized patients.

optic nerve – the connection between the eye and the brain.

patients – people being treated by medical practitioners such as nurses, doctors or physiotherapists.

pharmaceutical companies – organizations producing drugs for medical use.

physiotherapists – people trained to help patients who have physical disabilities or who have been ill, to get back the use of their bodies through doing exercises.

practice – the location or area in which doctors and other medical professionals work.

prescriptions – instructions for pharmacists from doctors, listing medicine to be given to patients.

psychiatrist – a doctor who specializes in mental health problems.

radiographer – medical professional who takes X-rays.

rural – to do with the countryside.

scaling – removing the stains and deposits on teeth.

scans – images of the body gained by using ultrasound or scanners.

sheltered accommodation – homes for people who need support with tasks such as shopping and cooking, or who need someone close by to make sure they are coping.

self-employed – working for yourself and doing jobs for several different people or organizations.

social workers – professionals trained to help people deal with difficulties, such as mental-health problems.

sterilizing – removing germs.

surgeon – doctor specializing in carrying out operations.

symptoms – signs of an illness, such as a high temperature.

therapists – people who treat conditions or problems in different ways. For example, an art therapist encourages patients to deal with their difficulties through art activities.

treatment – care given to a patient to make him or her well.

vision – eyesight.

X-rays – a stream of radiation passed into the body to reveal bones and different organs.

Further Information

So do you still want to work in healthcare?

This book does not aim to cover every job in healthcare, and many, including midwife and physiotherapist, are missing.

Working in healthcare involves helping people and this is very satisfying. But it is important to remember that the work can be tiring and the hours long. Not everyone can make a recovery, no matter how well they are cared for – healthcare workers need to be able to cope with this. And the work is often messy.

The way to decide if a job in healthcare is right for you is to find out as much as you can about such work. When you are old enough, you could think about doing voluntary work in a residential home or a day centre.

If you are at secondary school and seriously interested in a particular career, ask your careers teacher if he or she could arrange for some work experience. In this instance, this means spending some time, usually a week or two, in a hospital, a medical centre or a care home and this will show you what it is really like to work in healthcare.

Books

If you want to find out more about working in healthcare, you will find the following helpful:

A Career in Medicine: Do You Have What it Takes?, by Rameen Shakur, published by Royal Society of Medicine Press Ltd, 2006.

Careers in Medicine, Dentistry and Mental Health, by Loulou Brown, published by Kogan Page, 2000.

Careers and Jobs in Nursing, by Linda Nazarko, published by Kogan Page, 2004

Opportunities in Eye Care, by Linda Nazarko, published by McGraw-Hill Contemporary, 2001

Useful addresses

General

Prospects, the UK's official graduate careers website
www.prospects.ac.uk

Careers Scotland
www.careers-scotland.org.uk

Connexions Direct
www.connexions-direct.com

All healthcare careers

NHS Careers
PO Box 376
Bristol BS99 3EY
Tel: 0845 6060 655
www.nhscareers.nhs.uk

NHS Education for Scotland
22 Queen Street
Edinburgh EH2 1JX
Tel: 0131 226 7371
www.nes.scot.nhs.uk

Dentist

The British Dental Association
64 Wimpole Street
London
W1G 8YS
Tel: 0207 563 4545
www.bda.org

Doctor

British Medical Association
Tavistock Square
London
WC1H 9JP
Tel: 0207 387 4499
www.bma.org.uk

General Medical Council
Regent's Place
350 Euston Road
London NW1 3JN
Tel: 0845 357 3456
www.gmc-uk.org

Nurse

Nursing and Midwifery Council
23 Portland Place
London W1B 1PZ
Tel: 0207 637 7181
www.mnc-uk.org

Royal College of Nursing
20 Cavendish Square,
London W1G 0RN
Tel: 020 7409 3333
www.rcn.org.uk

Optician

Association of Optometrists
61 Southwark Street
London
SE1 0HL
Tel: 0207 261 9661
www.aop.org.uk

Pharmacist

The National Pharmacy Association
Mallinson House
38-42 St Peter's Street
St Albans
Hertfordshire AL1 3NP
Tel: 01727 832161
www.npa.co.uk

The Royal Pharmaceutical Society of Great Britain
Education Division
1 Lambeth High Street
London
SE1 7JN
Tel: 0207 735 9141
www.rpsgb.org.uk

Index